CW00429858

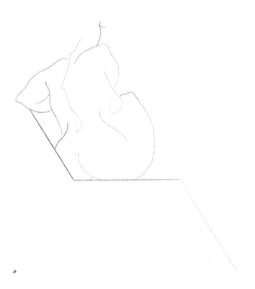

1

Miss Diagnosis

by

Molly Murray

A Collection of Poetry about Life with Chronic Illness

INDIGO COLLECTIVE
PRESS

INDIGO COLLECTIVE
PRESS

Indigo Collective Press
admin@indigocollectivepress.com
www.indigocollectivepress.com

ISBN: 9798716359352

Cover Illustration by Sophie Sturdevant
Typeset by Gordon Murray

Printed in the United Kingdom
First Edition 2021

www.mollymurrayhealingmagic.com

table of contents

dedication 7
bodies 11
elegies
elegies 15
flare 16
parasite 17
connoisseur 18
chronic warrior 20
writing on the
wall 22
sea monster 25
maelstrom 26
cyst 27
swell 28
blue genes 29
slip knot 30
body snatcher 31
white scars 32
chronic fatigue 34
dysfunction 36
lost soul 37
blur 38
bell curve 39
glisten 40
contrary 42
resistance 43
predatorial 44
drought 45
trè chic 46
sacrament
slow dance 48

devoid 50
60% chance 51
emergency
c section 52
untitled senryu 53
sacrament 54
fantasy
handful of air 58
firefly 59
forget-me-knot 60
wildwood 61
wild thing 62
force of gravity 64
help 66
fantasy 67
storytime
stigma 69
prescription 72
tapestry 73
waiting room 74
miss diagnosis 76
speed dating 78
my voice wears
leggings 80
my skeleton 84
the m.r.s. 85
relationship
issues 86
bananas 88
lichen 90
storytime 92

5

prologue
prologue 95
lost 97
winter seed 99
tbh with my
body 100
upstream 101
roots 102
hilary 103

topographical
map of self 104
stars 106
peace 108
celebration 109
invitation 110
exquisite 111
epilogue 112
ack. 115
biography 118

This collection is dedicated to me.

It's also dedicated to you.

Let's celebrate us.

WE ARE EXQUISITE.

Throughout my career, I have learned that fat bodies are inherently political.

~ Kelli Jean Drinkwater

TedX Sydney,
"Enough with the Fear of Fat," *May 2016.*

bodies

Every *body* has a story
legends buried by skin.

elegies

elegies

The cells hold room for grief,
writing elegies across my body
that ricochet in pain.

flare

A rope twisting
tighter, faster
dangling down the rock
wall of the cavern

I try to ease it
tangles, knots
hardens, wrenches
swinging, crashing –

I hold the fringes
of the rope with
fingertips – this will not
be an easy fall.

parasite

All the time,
like love or loss,
pain clings

to my limbs
invades my digits
my bloodstream

my self –
I can't identify
who I am

apart from
this mutant that
pain creates.

connoisseur

I stretch on my back,
describing
intricate,

delicate torture – nerves
needling
inside me

spiking through my
vulva. Inflammation
bludgeoning

my limbs with branches.
The wildfire
of the fascia

in my thoracolumbar
region. So many
shades of pain

a Pantone range of tones
saturating
the day

in vivid streaks, in all the
colors of the sea
and sky and earth,

every twinge its own,
remarkable
kaleidoscope.

chronic warrior

No sound
but the high pitch wing
of the bare
bow string

a caesura
in the song, wire taut to
detonate
with pain.

Air tense
with impending doom,
approaching
battle

the clash
imminent, my cells a
string of nerves,
my body

a battleground
of forces that the medical
field and I
do not understand.

writing on the wall

I dropped two things this morning,
(my child) (a milk jug)
fingers unfurling like fronds,

blue sky veins branching, palm
splaying back like a fern.
These fingers, this hand,

this arm – a Hallmark lesson of

death

universal and unremarkable

til it is scribbled on my own wall
during breakfast on a Saturday
morning, my toddler confused:
Mommy? Blue eyes looking up in
surprise.

The specialist couldn't say why
the artery died – it
seems reasonless

the way death strikes and takes
and takes and takes
what you love

your tabby cat, your future, your
child, your love. Today, this
moment,

a bone in my right wrist.
It shrivels, starved of nutrients,
turning gray, becoming ash
crumbling, crushed by the pressure
to survive.

Jagged trees of life spring from my
forearm
veins bulging, arrestingly bright,
that shocking
shade of late night eyeshadow and
tropical fish

screaming *poison! Toxic!* Neon blue
streaks
alarms bolting, screaming –

the emergency
response is slow, moseying along
without coffee,

no sense of urgency, what can it
do? Death
has already arrived.

sea
monster

a letter from my son

> *There is a sea*
> *monster in your belly.*

There is an
octopus

in your belly:
I saw her arms

coming out –
she is too big

to be inside.
There is a

plesiosaur
inside of you

trying to find home:
she wants to be free.

> *There is a sea*
> *monster in your belly.*

maelstrom

My
stomach is
an autocrat, forcing
my surrender to her
whims.

My
core is
always bruised, tender,
from the maelstrom confined
within.

cyst

Pressure.
Piercing.

Ribs spearing
through me
to my back.

Compression.
Sharp.

Devouring
me curled
up on my bed.

Agonizing.
Waiting.

Thinking we die
every day; some
days more than others.

swell

My body of water
is the Pacific,

a fluid flow expanding,
receding,

a tide of discomfort
too small,

too big

for one pair
of jeans.

blue genes

What, these genes?
I picked them up
second-hand.

They were left
behind in the gene
pool – obviously –

not anyone's first
choice with that
funky twist

of DNA. I got
the curvy wide-
leg from my dad

and the high-rise
hips from my mom.
I would've preferred

a smaller size – but
what can you do
about hand-me-downs?

s l i pkno t

Energy is a
slipknot
           receding

    under stress,
anxiety,
          exertion,

    releasing
the burden
        to the

    drop below.

body snatcher

Last night hovers
around me, a brute
that I can't shake

loping after me
relaxed, relentless,
stretching gray grapnel

to seize my mind
and motivation –
Who is this in my body?

An alien
peers through
the mirror.

white scars

My house key
slips from the mouth
of my velvet pocket.

I put down plastic
bags to sift, jostling
through the false hope

of debris in my hold–
all before I break
through the pane

to trespass my home.
Now broken glass
stares: a bandage

pasted on the gash
to heal the bleeding
of displacement.

It's not only keys.
In the scree of the murky
ago I've misplaced

irretrievable organs –
homes; memories; friends;
hope – I lose myself in a landslide

I can't express,
becoming less me as
I am swallowed

by pain, more this new person
who reveres each hair as it slips
laying like white scars

on her favorite sweater
clinging, phantom limbs
of amputation.

chronic fatigue

Sisyphus, king of
Corinth, trundling
the monolith up the
mountain, up, up –

imagine

the dips, the plateaus,
the relentless incline –
thin, sharp blade of air
grazing his throat

hammering

his agonized calves,
ripping his quadriceps
stone compressing his
wrists, arms, throttling

heartbeat,

clambering against
gods and wind to reach
the peak, to drop
his stone, to watch it

gyrate

down down down
to begin again, further
back than he began
never striding forward

without

falling behind –
condemned to
the agony of
everlasting

exhaustion.

dysfunction

scattered
        clustered
bewildered
        thoughts
throbbing
        flittering
bats
        in a belfry
betrayed
        bereft
by
        sleep.

lost sole

The
last
pair
in a
velvet
like
stand;
closet
heeled
I still
I slip

cascaded

blue glittered

vamp that made my shins look
Cat Woman's. I danced until I couldn't
I hobbled home barefoot, cast them in the
with forsaken rows of leather pumps and high-
boots I will not touch again. I miss them all –
feel the inflammation resonate in my bones as
on comfort soles and go out looking for myself.

blur

Clouds
            press close
    numbers
drift away
           names caught
    in the mist,
keys
           beyond my reach
    details snagged
in billows
           my mind,
    my life
snared
           by the
    brume.

bell curve

Wings. Rises. Soars. Skies.
Sharp. Curve.
Waves. Ocean. Depth. Drown.
Manic.

Manic.
Waves. Ocean. Depth. Drown.
Sharp. Curve,
Wings. Rises. Soars. Skies.

g l i s t e n

I have an
irrigation
system
of my own

no matter
what I do
do, how
slow I've run

how cold it is,
what icy
rain, what
gentle wind,

hot sweat
pours forth,
my hair
is drenched.

Men perspire,
ladies glisten,
but my glands re-
fuse to listen

I am always
full of dread
of the well-spring
in my head.

contrary

Coarse black horse hair stems
between my breasts
takes root

on my face sprouts
in hidden nooks
unwanted.

resistance

*"That's what happens when when you let yourself go:
greasy fries and Coca Cola, processed food
saturated fat and
sugars."*

No one
sees those hours –
the gym or sweat, tears
menu restrictions, medications,
constant exhausting battle to produce energy,
the fight for fitness or the struggle upstream for wellness,
only the visible torture summarized by two words: insulin resistance.

Visible torture summarized by two words: *insulin resistance*.
The fight for fitness, the struggle upstream for wellness
constant exhausting battle to produce energy
menu restrictions, the medications
the gym or sweat, tears.
No one sees those
hours.

predatorial

Ravenous, I saw
your wolf teeth baring within
you, hungry, ready

to clamp me
shred my organs, cut my veins
grow new through my blood

you rapacious
horde of carnivores prowling
round my naked cells.

drought

Desert sweeps
across your body

wells in your throat
desiccates your skin

your oasis is
parched

the dustbowl
of the great depression.

très chic

Medicate your pain
camouflage exhaustion
a modern woman.

sacrament

s low dance

You take your cue
acting on the beat

the rhythm of skin
jiving skin, our whole

in sync til the last
when we scale

to the peak and I
hold, pause, caesura

only breathe in arrest
for the climax that fails

to arrive while my body
wants, wills the release

the stress to cease,
while you hold me,

you hold me, you hold me,
you (sway) don't let go.

devoid

I
over
flow
with

desire

emptiness

pain

every
thing
but
life.

60% chance

We are all numbers,
all dancing on graphs

not knowing which lines
we are in, which totals

we become, dreading if
you will be, my precious

one –

the percentage that shreds
my body, heart and soul.

emergency
caesarian

No sound or breath at
the opening; only the
tense hush of waiting

once exigent knives
free your neck from the life cord
your lungs from poison.

My gaping self broke
for you, my son – breaks again
when you do not cry.

untitled senryu

They stole your body
from its burrow inside mine;
I hold a dark scar.

sacrament

We met at midnight
the red stains in the toilet
that were not welcome,
did not belong,
did not stop flowing
the pink souvenirs in my
panties were only
messengers.

And here you are
the smell of ancient rust
this turmoil in the pit of
my stomach
this dark red knot of
death:
all the hope inside of me.

Miscarriage, you are too clinical to
describe this sacred ritual
of delivering my child's
body to this knife of air
and water – this

sacrament

our bodies understand
while we watch from a
distance, baffled by the
divine mystery of breath,
soul, body, blood.

This was my birth.

A new mother, priestess,
woman, soul steps away
from this blood rite
the deep exhale of the
close of a journey.

I've let you pass but I
take you with me,
god-child, as I step
forward bathed in blood
and mystery, divine.

fantasy

handful of air

The fog descends
as you drift by
tattering my body
while you feast on the shreds.

I reach out, grasp weeds
on the bank, desperate
to catch a handful
of air from the light slipping past.

firefly

My boots caught in the
mudflats
tangled in rusty wire and
ancient
twine, slithering sand
yanking me down.

My hands grasped the
nothing
til they found a firefly, a
spark
reminding me to keep
trying –

we belong to wings and
flames.

forget-me-not

My thoughts dry, escape
a dandelion losing
florets to the wind.

wildwood

(As you can see)
my mind is brambles
a thorny tangled hedge
sparrow thoughts
escape.

wild thing

A wild creature lives
inside of
me.
She slipped in as a
little thing
not
asking for much but tea and soft
music,

nursing from my blood.

Now she's over-grown,
insatiable,
a beast
ripping her cage in pieces
detonating as she
paces,
claws, roars demanding
indefinable
peace.

I give her anything
everything
to make
my hands stop twitching
the wildcat
stop

shredding the walls.

force of gravity

It's heavier
than I
remembered.

Heavier
than anything
you could
benchpress
(if you
benchpressed)

heavier
than anything
we could survive

if it dropped
from a very
great height
down, fathoms,
eons, hurtling
with the force

of likelihood,
of facts, of
past experience,

of sleeplessness,
of trauma –
this monolith
– avalanche –
crushing
my mind.

help

Scrambling for a buzz

to stop the claws,
flashbacks

shredding me inside out.

fantasy

Diving from a waterfall like an island pearl fisher, my body melting away like a piece of silk. Arms above my head, swooping down, moments rushing beneath me, gushing into darkness and chaos, buried under acres of water. Time suspending, swinging, disappearing, sucked away. My body vanishing in the depth and the darkness; my body shredded, a stream of crimson silk glowing in black depths before it vanishes forever.

storytime

s t i gma

Sometimes an elephant
Traipses into the room
In between the frost and
Glances when I meet a
certain
Mindset and relaxes on
its haunches,
An awkward bulk by the
sofa.

prescription

He sits tapping his foot,
bored by the
symptoms

he ignores and the
complications tagging
along

dashing a few words
in bad script to describe
Hell

on a square
of white
paper.

tapestry

        In the tapestry
of my body,
        legends weave

together. All the
        threads of symptoms,
wafting in and out

        and in and
out create
        this magnificent

        complex of
mysteries that
        bind my body,

the skin
        unfurling
reveals

        dark pink
tissue,
        organs – a

story no
        one reads
but me.

waiting room

Every waiting room has
a blue lining:
wishful

thinking sits on the shelf
in bottles,
smudged

with thumbprints, too
many fingers here
before;

uncertainty crouches
beneath the
coffee

table, rests in orange chairs. The
door
swings –

the doctor peers in.
She wears
only

sterile disinterest, her
face papered
with

disbelief, her gloves
smell of dust
and

dispassion: hope smashes
on the tile
floor.

miss diagnosis

I won't compare myself
to Sleeping Beauty but I
could say I'm like her
castle:
buried in an intricate
maze
of thorny symptoms
incestuously feeding
from each other.
Am I a princess
masked inside chaos
in a tower doctors can't
find?

In a tower doctors
can't find
masked inside chaos
I am the princess
of thorny symptoms
incestuously feeding
from each other
buried in an intricate
maze
I could say I'm
Sleeping Beauty or
the castle –
I won't compare
my self.

speed dating

I'd like to invite you
to a speed dating event
for doctors.

I don't have the time
or energy or interest
for a sip of Shiraz-Cab

in the horde who put my
symptoms in Ziploc bags
labelled "Women's

Issues" and "Obese." I'm
not interested in
misogynists who bill me

for assuming they are
capable of "fixing" me
with a one-size-fits-all

pill for speedy (weight) loss
that sends me rushing to the Ladies'
Room where he or she

believes I belong. I want
no more than the
satisfaction of a chance

to tell them all to their
flaccid faces:
No thanks. Moving on.

my voice wears leggings

I plan moments in which
I'm not in bed
writhing

plotting my plan of
survival between
pills

insurance quotas, signatures
and disbelief,
the proper

amount of business days
to lapse between
refills

according to politicians at the
beck and call of the
dictatorship

of cold hard cash, kissing
the asses of FDA-
approved

drug lords, pharmaceutical
führers exterminating
victims

by coercion insurance moguls
and my doctor, who
is fearful

of healing me and losing her own
stash of cash – everyone,
everywhere

choreographed to the cacophonous
clash of cash,
healthcare

campaigning against me to cover
their own backends
by cutting off

the end of this chain of cash
and command,
the base

of their pyramid, chronic pain
patients caught in this
nightmare –

they only want to survive – to
function – to take
their toddlers

to the park and the grocery –
to get out of bed in
the morning

would it be too much to dream
of keeping a job or
working out?

But why take my word for it?
Unlike the FDA, unlike
politicians,

unlike capitalists, my voice
is notorious for
exaggeration.

My voice is historically in-
accurate. My voice is
ignorant. My voice

is not to be trusted. My voice
is unpopular. My voice is
exhausted. My voice

is shrill. My voice is fat.
My voice is curvy.
My voice wears

leggings. My voice is in
pain. My voice is
uncomfortable.

My voice is a woman's voice.

my skeleton

My skeleton in the closet
        circles every first
                glass of wine,
        every first kiss.
When do I tell?

First, second, third date
        becomes never
                our relationship
        falters, jolts.

When I lean on his shoulder
        the scars of harassment
                and injury slip by
        but not the panic
of my escaping hair

or even the innocent fact that
        my body cannibalizes its
                own muscle to move
        or that energy is a ticking
grenade or the future of diabetes
and improbable offspring –

no, I think that can wait.

the m.r.s.

metabolic reproductive syndrome
aka PCOS

My other half
        is the evil one

the one you don't want
        to run into in the grocery

store the one that will
        keep you up late at night

make you gain stress-weight,
        the one that wears you out

until even your exhaustion feels
        tired. She'll send you to the

clinic and the bottle. She'll tie you
        up in knots – tear out your

hair – pock your skin – make you
        ache in every part of your

body – I'm telling you, you don't
        want to meet the M.R.S.

relationship
issues

My body is a liar –
       cheating hoe!
never listens, hurts
me in return

for compliments
       gives me exhaustion
when I give her rest
gives me reserves

of fat when I give her
       famine, never logs in my
dairy, wheat and sugar free
menu, hangs out in public

saying she is unloved,
        uncared for though I lavish
her with attention, tenderness
money to make her beautiful.

My body is a dealer
        gone dirty: she denies me
insulin when I'm dying.
My body is a liar.

bananas

I feel bananas
longingly in the produce
aisle.

Research changes
every season with the produce,
the satsumas roll in,

the data rolls out.
I read a fresh set
of conclusive evidence

and understand why
tomatoes hurt my stomach
and what was once

a superfood is now a super
villain – take the watermelon
forget the varieties of lettuce

shifting in and out.
Don't even start
the conversation

about red wine and dark
chocolate – don't talk
to me about grapes!

There is a communication
breakdown in my body;
but the research is 20

years behind. I am lost
in the grocery store, in
the labyrinth of misleading

statistics, and while
the veg grows mold
I feel bananas.

l i chen

The green nesting
tangled in itself
is a coiled composition
of perfect imperfection;

tangled in itself
lichen grasps its precious spirals
of perfect imperfection
unanchored but unchanged.

Lichen grasps its precious spirals,
each fragile branch
unanchored but unchanged,
invulnerably green.

Each fragile branch
huddling in the storm,
invulnerably green,
pummeled by the squall.

Huddling in the storm
I'm wind-stretched
pummeled by the squall,
bare-boned and battered-flat.

I'm wind-stretched,
word-whipped and steamrolled,
bare-boned and battered-flat –
I miss my shape.

Word-whipped and steamrolled,
I've lost the one I was before the
blitz – I miss my shape,
My wild and carefree shape.

I've lost the one I was before the
blitz – the green-nesting,
wild and carefree shape
tangled in itself,

The green-nesting,
coiled composition
tangled in itself
of perfect imperfection.

s t o r y t ime

Every body has a story –
        a sad past climbing with big
        bad wolves and evil
            stepmothers

propogating like cockroaches.
        Injuries, diseases, are so
        much easier to accept when
        they come

wrapped in a myth or a fairytale
        villain, instead of being the
        cannibalistic bastards
        they are

chewing your future and present
        happiness from the inside,
        an invisible coup
        d'états;

just remember when you see me,
        me, her, him, you crawling
        and lumbering,
                heaving

a disfigured self past, when
        you think: why would she
        let herself go? he
                needs to hit

the gym – lay off
        the sweets – grow
        some new hair, skin,
                a new self –

every body has a story.

prologue

prologue

Every time I die
I birth a new self

every shadow death
leads me here

this ready moment, this
blank page.

lost

Find her in the long
grass with the roots and stones
where
you last saw yourself.

winter seed

Roots stretch deep
a green stalk rises

your voice blazes
through the silence

breaking the rock
dark winter soil.

tbh with
my body

I hated you

in high school. You didn't look
like anyone else; you were
awkward, uncomfortable beneath
your skin.

I really, really hated you

for what you did to me in social
situations, the way you looked to
me to somehow save you from
yourself.

I realize

my soul is shallow to
judge you by my eyes; I
need to give you the
grace you give me,

carrying me broken
through this broken life.

upstream

Let go
of the scars
they burned into you

watch them
drift away like
feathers.

roots

The
maple in
our backyard loses
itself in curls, shavings
falling

like
memories in
the grass round
its trunk. Roots never
change.

hilary

Shoots
thriving in
frozen fields, held –
hidden – fast by secret
strength.

topographical
map of self

There are moguls –
        bumps in the path,
slashes from friends

        gashes from stigma
and religion became
        this endless black ravine

not to mention
        the Grand Canyon
of break ups

        the ash hills
dead earth
        where I burn

the lava bed, still
          smoldering, kindled
by chronic disease

and injury, endless
          seas, sand dunes
cast by wind and tide

a landscape shaped
          by a deluge of pain. From
this view,

the scenery takes my breath.

s t a r s

His tiny baby fingers
       fumble for stickers
from the sheet of stars

bright pinks, blues,
       greens, yellows
that he firmly,

so carefully,
       so gently,
presses onto

my tummy.
       The baby weight
the endo weight

the pcos weight
        the cystitis weight
the weight of

all the baggage
        I let define
me rolling off

I let it go
        my stomach
is covered

in stars and scars
        and kisses
and I accept

this gift of love.
        I take in this
gift of stars.

peace

Strolling storm-tossed
sand, sifting
seaweed, sea glass

treasuring
my scallop shell
of quiet.

celebration

Here's to the girl
I don't know.

The one who spends
every penny

of herself, but can't
get out

of bed; highest when
she is lowest,

running hardest – pushing,
working, sweating –

to run at all – here's
to the girl

I am trying to learn,
learning to love

let's celebrate her.
Celebrate me.

intuition

The board slips,
splintering

I ease this weight
into my heels

one step – slowly –
after another

the boards growing
secure, steady,

I build this bridge
as I walk across it

trusting my own
fluid magic

stronger, constant
with every step.

exquisite

Guard
your soul
preciously –
it's the only
one.

epilogue

The average years before diagnosis,
and

the average cost of diagnosis,
misdiagnosis, and mis-medication,
and

the average number of bodies with
mystery conditions or with
untreatable conditions

is extravagant.

Extravagant.

The toll of medical gaslighting
on the mental health and emotional
health of individuals
suffering with these conditions is
extravagant.

The toll on human life is
extravagant.

I see you. I hear you. I believe you.

You are exquisite.

One day the medical patriarchy will come crumbling down

One day we will trust our bodies

we will respect our stories

and other people will trust and respect them the same way.

you are extravagantly beautiful.

acknowledgements

Body Snatcher. *Fearsome Critters*. Vol. 1.

Chronic Fatigue. *Three Drops in a Cauldron*. May 2019.

Cyst. *Herstry*. Nov. 5, 2018.

Drought. *Herstry*. Nov. 5, 2018.

Elegies. *Tiny Spoon*. Issue 4.

Emergency Caesarian. *ByMePoetry WOMb*. 2018.

Firefly. *A Walk with Nature: Poetic Encounters that Nourish the Soul*. University Professors Press. 2019.

Handful of Air. *Herstry*.
Nov. 5, 2018.

Lichen. *The Wayfarer*.
Vol. 5, Issue 2.

Predatorial. *Three Drops
in a Cauldron*. May 2019.

Prescription. *Minnie's
Diary*. 2019.
**Nominated for a 2019
Pushcart Prize.**

Stigma. *By Me Poetry
America*. Featured Poet.
May 4, 2017.

Storytime. *Reapparition
Journal*. Issue 1.

Swell. *Harness Magazine*.
March 2020.

TBH with my Body.
Reapparition Journal.
Issue 1.

Très Chic. *Bonsai*. Vol. 1.

Topographical Map of
Self. *Reapparition Journal.*
Issue 1.

Untitled Senryu.
ByMePoetry WOMb. 2018.

Upstream. *Tiny Spoon.*
Issue 4.

Waiting Room. *The
Puffin Review.* Issue 10.

Wildwood. *Tiny Spoon.*
Issue 4.

60%. *Herstry.* Nov. 5,
2018.

biography

Molly Murray is a mum, a writer, and a transformation coach. In her former life, she was a spoonie, a chronic warrior, and a survivor of severe trauma.

A few years ago, she found herself in such severe pain that her life was completely paused. Around the same time, she realized that she was in a downward spiral of trauma – for every step forward, she felt like she took two steps back. She was losing hope of ever climbing out.

She manifested healing from the pain and trauma, and manifested a new life living in her dream house on a beach doing what she loves.

Now, she guides people to heal from trauma and manifest a life they love through private coaching and her course, Manifest Healing.

Molly writes poetry and Middle Grade Fantasy that builds bridges and creates a sense of wonder and empathy.

Her pieces are widely published, including by *Litro*, *The Wayfarer*, *The Curlew* and many others (including *Third Wednesday* – where she will never forget that her poem was published on the page after Ted Kooser's). One of her poems was nominated for a 2019 Pushcart prize.

She is passionate about breaking stereotypes and letting the light in to broken places.

Find Molly on Instagram & Facebook
IG: @exlibrismollymurray.
FB: facebook.com/groups/
manifesthealingnow.

You can find her freebies, books, and courses, or reach out to her for coaching or speaking engagements, through her website:
mollymurrayhealingmagic.com

Printed in Great Britain
by Amazon

17708327R00071